MY SON
PHILLIPE

MY SON PHILLIPE

Nadia Herndon

ARPress
ILLUMINATING IDEAS
EMPOWERING VOICES

ARPress
45 Dan Road Suite 36
Canton MA 02021

Hotline: 1(888) 821-0229
Fax: 1(508) 545-7580

Ordering Information:
Quantity Sales. Special discounts are available on quantity purchases by corporations, associations, and others. For details, contact the publisher at the address above.

Printed in the United States of America.

ISBN-13   Paperback   979-8-89356-285-9
              eBook   979-8-89356-284-2

Library of Congress Control Number: 2024903448

For my son Phillipe Reznitsky, husband John Koss,
and all the people who stood by us during the time of our hardship.

Thank you.

Contents

Cast

The President of the United States: Mr. Ronald Reagan The Honorable Senator of Alaska: Mr. Ted Stevens The staff assistant of Ted Stevens's office in the United States Senate: Mrs. Johnson The American Veteran of War: Mr. John Koss Phillipe Habib: Sir Phillipe Reznitzky, Alaskan Alaskan Poet: Miss Nadia Phillip (mother of Sir Phillipe Reznitsky) The Rabbi: name unknown The Russian Artist: Leonid Reznitsky (the Grandpa) The King of Jordan: Mr. Abdullah (the patron of the St. Bethany School) The principle of Saint Bethany boarding school for girls: Mother Sophie The Jordanian guide and the donkey: names unknown Two United Nations paramedics: names unknown The owners of the Arabian Hotel in Jerusalem: names unknown The Chief Speaker of the International Christian Embassy in Jerusalem: Mr. Van der Hoven The Minister of Defense of Israel: Ariel Sharon The leader of Palestinian uprising: Mr. Yasser Arafat The Israeli Ambassador in the United States: name unknown The American Ambassador in Israel: name unknown The Chinese cook in Jerusalem: name unknown The personal pilot of the US President: name unknown The agent of New York Life Insurance Agency: Mr. Robert Barrett, Jr. The Chair of the Department of Foreign Languages of UAA: Dr. Margaret Engel The secretaries of the Embassies: names unknown The secretary of the US President and his bodyguards: names unknown The Israeli Security: names unknown.

Act I

Captain Cook Hotel.
Anchorage, Alaska.

Scene 1: Captain Cook Hotel.

The snow blizzard is in its power. It throws snowflakes and blows crystals of ice, which sparkle like precious stones. The wind is singing like the ancient shamans. It grasps the coats, scarves, and hats of the guests who are trying to enter the hotel. The paintings of "Village Arabe" by Israeli artist Andrey Reznitsky are nicely displayed. These are original paintings of landscapes in pastel. It's a series of twelve landscapes depicting the same Arabian village, Hizma, during different times of the day. Due to different lighting, not a single picture seems alike. They are of the same size: 99 x 48.24 cm, painted circa 1984. The landscapes were exhibited at "The House of Artists" in 1984 in Jerusalem, Israel, during "One Man Show of Andrey Reznitsky." They were later displayed in Paris, France and Fairbanks, Alaska. The paintings have been placed into the custody of Mr. Phillipe Reznitsky, the son of the artist, who has been preserving them with a lot of care.

Today, Phillipe and his mom Nadia have displayed them for the first time in Anchorage, in an effort to promote education for the Alaskan people. A group of musicians are playing the music of Beethoven. White roses, candles, and a very exquisite buffet are making a pleasant addition to the vernissage. The guests are pouring into the auditorium, like springs into the ocean. They are greeted by a tall, athletic gentleman in a very elegant grey suite: Mr. Phillipe Reznitsky, the son of the artist.

He is escorting them to the paintings, answering their questions, and answering phone calls from acquaintances, clients, and the guests. Even the White House has called, and they said: "We wish you the best."

Mr. Robert Barrett and the mother of Phillipe are quietly sitting at the table. They are talking like two old friends.

Nadia: Robert, it's so nice of you to come to see Phillipe and the paintings. That awful blizzard stopped so many people from coming... Phillipe has worked so hard to make that vernissage. He even sold his only vehicle to cover the expenses, so that the people of Alaska could see and enjoy these magnificent paintings of his father.

Robert: Yes, they are very special. So much talent...and the colors create such mystique, just like Jerusalem. I also like the portrait of the Prime Minister of Israel, Menachem Begin; it's the only one in the world. Is there any way that you can tell me about the creation of that portrait?

Nadia: Well, at that time, we all had been residing in Jerusalem. Andrey was working as a graphic artist with one of the publishing houses. He joined the Union of Israeli Artists, and I worked as an art manager for one of the art galleries. One of my colleagues introduced us to the son of the chief Rabbi of Belgium, David, who commissioned Andrey to make the oil portrait of his mother, who perished in a Nazi concentration camp during the war. David built a school in the memory of his mother and wanted to have her portrait there. All he had was a tiny photograph in black and white. There wasn't any other image available. Andrey worked for nine months to create that portrait.

Robert: For nine months! How could anyone survive nine months in Israel without pay?

Nadia: Just like all the other artists do: on bread and water. David liked the portrait a lot. He had a good friend, Mr. Menachem Begin, who suggested that Andrey make his oil portrait. We accepted the proposal. It was another nine months of intensive work. We were allowed to work with the archives of the Prime Minister and come to his office any time. Creating the portrait was part of a fundraising campaign: David was to print the posters from the portrait, which were scheduled to be sold overseas, and the funds from the sale were designated to build a hospital for children in Jerusalem.

Robert: Gosh, Nadia, it's all so interesting. I am going closer to the portrait and would like to be photographed right next to it. It's not every day that we can have our picture with the Prime Minister!

Robert walks to Phillipe and the portrait. The photographer takes their photo. Phillipe continues to host the guests. They all admire the paintings and express their gratitude to Phillipe for the nice event.

Robert comes back to Nadia.

Robert: Nadia, can you tell us about the landscapes? How were they created and how did they make it across the Atlantic to Alaska?

It becomes very quiet.

Nadia: When our son was young—twenty years ago—one summer night, it was decided that he would travel to Jerusalem to visit his father and his family. It all happened twenty years ago. It all began in Anchorage at the International Airport in the terminal next to Alaska Airlines....

Act II

International Airport Named after Ted Stevens. Anchorage, Alaska.

Scene 1: International airport.

John Koss, his stepson Phillipe Reznitsky, and his wife Nadia Phillips are at the airport terminal next to the Alaska Airlines boarding zone. It's a quiet summer evening. Geese are seen through the large airport windows. They are preparing for migration to far lands in the anticipation of the coming winter. They outcry their songs, and the deep violet colors of the sky are gradually turning into dark, velvet night. There is a lot of sorrow in their songs: Phillipe is going to travel to Jerusalem to visit his father and his family. John, Phillipe, and Nadia are sitting on the bench and are listing to the geese. John suddenly breaks the silence and talks very emotionally.

John (emotionally): Nadia, I still think that Phillipe should stay home here in Alaska. It's a very dangerous land, Israel. It's like stepping into the minefields. I am worried about Phillipe. He hasn't been in combat. He is too young to be there, and it's a very long voyage. I am begging you on my knees. Don't send the child there.

He gets on his knees in front of Nadia. He is crying.

Nadia: John, please stop. Phillipe hasn't seen his father, his grandpa, his brother, and his sister for so many years. Can't you understand how important it is to be with family? Phillipe will meet with his new friends and the people of Jerusalem. He can see the Holy Land and learn a lot about the different religions and cultures. It's a dream vacation. Why do you want to deprive the child of such happiness, such a rare opportunity to be with the family and to experience the treasures of the Bible Land? Travelling expands the horizons; it opens the mind. It's very educational. You don't have a heart, John!

She turns away from John and kisses Phillipe on the nose.

Nadia: Phillipe, honey, do you miss your poodle? You called her, "*Achshafat Hashmal*" (*Hebrew for dark as the night without any electricity*). Do you remember your nickname, "Phillipe Habib?" Yes, that's what everybody called you. You were the only blond child in Jerusalem. They all have black, curly hair. They all loved you.

John: He was only four years old. What can he remember? The kid is scared. Can't you see how pale he is?

Phillipe: I am not scared. I am not just anybody. I am an Alaskan. I really don't remember too much, Mommy. Do they have "Fred Meyers" there?

Nadia: I don't know what they have now. It was so long ago that we were there. But when you come back, we'll go to "Fred Meyers" and "Chucky Cheese." We shall dance with Chucky, and then we shall celebrate "Halloween" and wear funny costumes. What costume would you like to wear, son?

Phillipe: I want to be GI-Joe. I also want to buy for you "Lee Press-On Nails." Then you will have long, long nails, just like my friend's mom.

John (smiling through his tears): Phil, you have a good flight. Don't worry about the "Lee Press-On Nails." I'll buy them for Christmas. Do you need anything for Christmas?

Phillipe: I already wrote a letter to Santa Clause. But my friend Frank wants something. I'll tell you when I come.

The escorting flight attendants pick up Phillipe. They disappear inside of the plane. The sky and everything around become very dark.

An enormous fear grasps the heart of Nadia.

Nadia: Why do I have such fear? Why is it so dark? Why is Death driving in the carriage and laughing at me? John, have you seen it?

John: What do you want me to see, Nadia? I made the arrangements for Phillipe to start training with the cadets to prepare him for West Point. And now he is gone. We shall never see him again. One day, you will be very sorry for what you have done: You've sent your only friend, Phillipe, to the war zone. There is always the war there—always. Phillipe loves you more than anything in the world, and you just sent him to nowhere.

Nadia: There isn't any war there, John; it's the imagination of your mind. You were wounded while in combat. You and your partner encountered a mine. It exploded. You carried your partner to safety while your own belly was being torn apart. You wake up Phillipe and me in the night because you scream in your dreams. Your body is here, but you are not. It's scary to live with a man like you. There are lots of flowers in Jerusalem; it's very peaceful. People sell falafels. Phillipe loves falafels.

John: Really? What about living with a woman like you? You are either with Leo Tolstoy or with that Spaniard—what's his name?

Nadia: Federico Garcia Lorca, the great Spanish poet. He actually likes my poetry a lot.

John: These people are dead, Nadia. They cannot read your poetry. It's you who lives in the world of the dreams. I don't even know why I am here….

Nadia: John, can you please—pretty please—stop that airplane? That lady in the carriage…she is following them. It's she—Death!

John: First you want to send your kid to Jerusalem, and then you want me to stop the airplane. Nobody can stop that plane now—nobody.

Act III

The House of the Artist Reznitsky.
Jerusalem, Israel.

Scene 1: The house of the artist Reznitsky.

The stepmother, father, and his son Phillipe have just arrived at their house from Ben Gurion International Airport. They have travelled almost two hours by bus and are very tired. The house is under repair. There are construction materials and buckets with paint everywhere. The windows are half done. There are no doors. The grandfather is standing on the steps of the house, holding in his arms the younger brother of Phillipe. It is the holy day Purim. The kid and grandfather are dressed as characters from that ancient Hebrew epos, and so are the neighbors and the people of Jerusalem. They are celebrating that festivity vigorously.

Grandpa: Phillipe, here is your younger brother Kiril. He was born here after you and your mom already went to America. Welcome back home. Kiril, say hi to your brother Phillipe.

Kiril spits into the face of Phillipe. Phillipe immediately spits back into the face of Kiril. Everyone is in shock, especially Phillipe.

Stepmother: Kiril is just a kid, Phillipe. He really didn't mean to insult you. He is actually very glad to see you.

Phillipe: I don't like your son, Eada. We do not spit into the faces of our guests. That's very rude. I travelled all the way here to tell you that you are nothing but dust under my sandals. My mom has better hair than you. You stole my father from me. You are the thief; that's what you are!

Everybody goes into even bigger shock. Eada grabs Kiril and runs from the house. Andrey runs after them. Only Phillipe and the grandpa remain at the stairs.

Grandpa: Well, we didn't expect you to arrive so soon. The house is under construction, but we arranged a room for you, the one your mother lived in when she was here. Her library is still there, as is her embroidery. We bought falafels and textbooks for you. Your father enrolled you into the special school named after Ben Gurion. He had to go up to Knesset to acquire a place at that school for you. Eada is a Zionist, and she wants to raise you as a Zionist, too.

Phillipe becomes very angry.

Phillipe: I don't want to hear about your Eada. I don't know what "Zionist" means. I don't want to attend your schools. I will never stay here. I only came to look into the face of your son Andrey and to tell him that I cried so many days and nights because he left me as if I am nothing—as if my mom is nothing. I want to tear all the hair in his beard.

Phillipe begins to shake and starts sobbing bitterly.

Phillipe: *Aba Shely*, why did you leave me?

The grandpa rushes to Phillipe and tries to press him to his chest.

Grandpa: Child, don't talk that way about your father. Your father loves you. I love you. You are too young to understand yet. One day you will grow up, and you will be proud of your daddy. He is such a talented artist. He…

Phillipe pushes aside his grandpa.

Phillipe: I am not a child. I am a man. You don't even have a house. It's just a construction site. You don't even have doors on that place.

Phillipe pushes away his grandpa and runs into the streets of Jerusalem. People are singing and dancing. They try to dance with Phillipe, but he runs and runs. He is lost in that city. He falls on the hill and cries bitterly. He takes the dust from the road and puts it on his head and all over his face. He sees a lonely flower and stands on his knees in front of it.

Phillipe: Mama. Mama!

Andrey and Eada call the police and ask them to find Phillipe. As the days go by, they continue to look for Phillipe. Nobody knows where he sleeps or what he eats.

Policeman: Children, they are American flowers. They cannot be planted on the rocks of Jerusalem. Where did you get the idea to bring that kid here? As if we don't have enough trouble with the Palestinians…

The night falls on Jerusalem. It's cold—very cold in the night.

Scene 2: Split view: the interiors of Andrey's house and the American house, where John and Nadia are on phone.

John and Nadia call to see how Phillipe is doing. Eada comes to the phone.

Eada: Phillipe? Oh, he is just fine. He already took a shower and ate his dinner. Yes, he ate a lot of falafels. And he is already sleeping. Shalom.

Scene 3: A dark house on the outskirts of Jerusalem.

Two men with kerchiefs on their heads, which are covering their faces, are dragging Phillipe by the hair up and down the stairs—up and down. A third man runs to them.

Third man: Stop dragging that kid. He is not Jewish. Leave him alone. He is almost dead. His weight is only fifty pounds. Even the dogs wouldn't eat him. We have to get ready for the uprising. It starts tomorrow morning.

First man: What about the kid? Should we drop him near the American Embassy, or should we ask for a ransom?

Third man: Let the Americans worry about their kids. They will find him if they want him.

They disappear into the darkness.

A street dog comes to Phillipe and starts licking his face. Phillipe opens his eyes and puts his arms around the neck of the dog. It has very long hair, and it wraps Phillipe into it. He hides his face in its belly and falls asleep.

Scene 4: An aerial view of Jerusalem.

A blizzard is rampaging the city. The cold wind is moaning like the jackals, and all the buildings are painted in black paint. All the windows are covered by cartons, and the Palestinians, with their faces covered by traditional scarves, are sitting atop the roofs with rocks in their hands. They stone to death anyone who dares to step into the streets. Phillipe is pressing his slim body next to the wall of one of the buildings. His clothes are now pure rags; he is just skin and bones. His tiny body is covered by wounds and lice; he is hardly alive. An explosion across the street rips apart the body of a suicide bomber. His blood and pieces of his body are falling on Phillipe. Phillipe is horrified. He doesn't cry anymore or call for his mom. Phillipe is just standing and very sadly looking into the darkness, where far away beyond the rivers, lakes, and mountains on the other part of the globe is that beautiful peaceful, unreachable land: Alaska. He is about to step into the street, so that the Palestinians could see him. He wants to die under their rocks. He is so lonely and unhappy that he thinks that it's better to die than to live like that.

A Chinese man runs from his restaurant. He picks up Phillipe and carries him away from the streets into the safety of the restaurant. Phillipe loses consciousness. The Chinese man is crying.

Chinese man: Kid! Kid, don't die.

He wraps him in blankets and is holding his tiny hands in his arms.

Chinese man: Where is your mommy? Where is your daddy?

There is no answer.

A white seagull flies from the roof, through a window and into the sky— far into the darkness. It becomes bigger and bigger. And soon it covers the sky.

The Angel spreads his mighty wings, with his feathers softer than silk.

Angel: I will shake entire earth for every tear that you have dropped.

Chinese man: What is your name?

Phillipe (in a whisper): Phillipe—Habib.

Phillipe loses consciousness.

The Chinese man presses Phillipe to his heart. It's very dark at the restaurant. One can hear the snowstorm, the explosions, and the sounds of shrapnel and bullets. Another long, cold, and merciless night comes to Jerusalem.

Phillipe sees a dream: He and his mother are at McDonalds in Anchorage. He jumps into the pool of the colorful balls. His mother is looking for him everywhere. A white donkey appears, and Phillipe climbs on the donkey.

Phillipe: I love you, donkey. And I want to give you a big hug and kiss.

Act IV

University of Alaska. Anchorage.

Scene 1: The University of Anchorage, Alaska.

A blizzard throws snowflakes into the face of Nadia. She helplessly stands next to the building. A bird strikes the stainless glass of the dark structure and drops dead next to her feet. She picks up the bird, which is still warm but already not breathing. She sees her son Phillipe standing in the streets of Jerusalem. He is just like the ghost. He doesn't have any coat and is very cold. His body is covered by wounds. All buildings are painted in black paint. The windows are sealed by piles of wood. Phillipe doesn't cry anymore. He just stands there and very sadly looks into the eyes of Nadia. She falls on her knees.

Nadia (screaming): Oh no! No!

Dr. Margaret Engel runs to Nadia.

Margaret: What's wrong? Why are you crying and screaming? I don't want our students to see you crying. I don't want anybody to see you crying! We are in the middle of the semester, and we have such great enrollment. There is a proposal for you to translate the science research of the cartographer Gvozdev, the land surveyor and the explorer. There is a proposal to train the administrators of Federal Aviation in Russian. They are working to open the flying routes from Alaska to the Russian Far East, and you are assigned to be their translator. Yours is a high, rocketing career, and you are standing and crying here! What are you crying about?

Nadia (shaking): *Eled Shely* (Hebrew for "my beloved son"), Phillipe. People are writing with blood on the walls of Jerusalem!

Margaret: What are they writing?

Nadia: Antifada.

Margaret calls John.

Margaret: John, come at once to the University. Nadia has too much stress. She had a vision of her son, and she is not herself. She says that people are writing "antifada" with blood on the walls of Jerusalem. She called there already five times, and she is crying all the time. Do something. The Dean will cut off my head if we don't make it through semester. Take her to dinner, take her shopping, shower her with gifts, or put her on "Prozac" medication. Just don't leave her alone for even a minute. But we must complete the semester. And bring her to Federal Aviation tomorrow by nine. The Russians are cooperative: They are willing to open flight routes to Anadyr, Chabarovsk, and Vladivostok. Their delegation is already here. Nadia is magnificent when she talks to them. They are fascinated by her Russian. They wrote already three letters of gratification to our department.

John: I don't think that shopping is going to help here. She has refused to eat for several days already. She is devastated by this separation with her son. Some women go insane when they are separated from their children. I am not a psychiatrist, but I agree: We should take her to the doctor right now. I don't give a damn about the delegations. They should bring their own interpreters with them. And as for your classes, you should give her at least an assistant. She is exhausted from checking the homework of the students. You have been slaving her day and night. I am not surprised that she is on the verge of insanity. What I am surprised about is that she lasted so long. Get the military linguists from Fort Richardson for the negotiations, and I'll nail your Dean to the wall if you don't get an assistant for her by tomorrow and another one for the science translation on the land surveyor Gvozdev. It was published by the Academy of Science, and it requires the Academy of Science from our side, too. I am through with you, Margaret. End of conversation.

Scene 2: Nadia and John's apartment.

Nadia and John live in a modest apartment in the Muldoon area of Anchorage. The clock strikes midnight. Nadia is sitting at the table and translating the science book. She writes page by page. The tears are streaming down her cheek. All the pages are covered with her tears.

Nadia: John, I am very tired. I want to go to the store to buy some snacks. I'll be right back.

John: Well, I am tired too. That's all right to go to the store. Just put a coat on. There's a blizzard happening. But remember, if you are not back within thirty minutes, I'll call the cops. You will not run away too far from here. I told you not to send the kid to Jerusalem, but you wouldn't listen to me. They have just broadcasted in the news that the Palestinian uprising broke off in Jerusalem. They said it was called "antifada." The United Nations sealed the borders to prevent the conflict from spreading any further. We cannot get your kid to Anchorage now. All the airplanes are grounded. To disobey a guy like me…you have no blood or money in my country. I shed my blood for it. And when we tell you something, you should listen to us and obey. Even our President Roosevelt listened to me, but you didn't. And now we'll see how that Spaniard, Federico, is going to help you. You may go to the store now. Thirty minutes—that's all you have. And then you may have some rest. At nine o'clock, I will deliver you for translations. We have orders to open the air routes with the Far East. I love you, Nadia, but I love my country, too. And I will bring you to that negotiation, dead or alive. No, I will not stand on my knees today in front of you. We shall not stand on our knees in front of anybody. Your Prime Minister Chrushev said that you would be dancing on our graves. Go and dance now.

John goes into the bedroom and slams the doors. Nadia runs from the apartment into the blizzard. The snow banks are almost up to her waist. She falls into the snow and then gets up again and again. She runs to the airport. The airline counter clerk is horrified when she steps inside.

Scene 3: Airport.

Airline clerk: Oh my God, what do you want?

Nadia: An airline ticket to Jerusalem, please.

Airline clerk: What a strange request! Everybody wants a ticket from Jerusalem to America at this time, and you want a ticket to Jerusalem!

Nadia: I am a mother. My kid is there. Are you a mother?

Airline clerk: Yes. Yes, if my kid was there, I would go there, too.

Act V

Israeli Embassy. New York.

Scene 1: Israeli Embassy.

New York is all covered with snow. It's very cold. Nadia is all the time shaking; she is emotionally exhausted. She knows that John, the police, and the FBI are already looking for her everywhere. She wonders if she should hide in the snowbank and rest there until morning, or if she should find the Israeli Embassy tonight. Her feet are wet. It feels like there are fifty pounds attached to each of them. She wonders if she should take off her boots, since they are so heavy. She tries to pull them off. Alas, her feet are swollen, and the boots keep them inside with an iron grip.

She arrives at the Embassy. It's already dark. They are going to be closed in fifteen minutes. Nadia makes a final effort and steps in. The Embassy staff is in shock. They don't know what to do: to call the paramedics or to call the police.

Nadia (speaking to one of them): Ambassador, I ought to talk to you now.

Ambassador (stunned): How do you know that I am the Ambassador? Please, be quiet.

He walks her into his office.

Ambassador: Ma'am, what's the matter? Who told you about my rank? Are you a secret agent or a terrorist?

Nadia: Neither nor.

She can hardly stand on her feet. Nadia tells him exactly what happened: how she sent her son for the dream vacation, how her former husband refused to give him back, and how she saw the vision. She begs the Ambassador to help her to get to Jerusalem. As she talks, she keeps on crying. The Ambassador calls to the house of Andrey and talks to him. Ambassador tells Nadia "Hu lo rotzé" (Hebrew "He doesn't want")

Ambassador: Hu Lo Rotze' *(Hebrew for He doesn't want).*

Nadia: I just want my son.

The Ambassador covers his face with his hands.

Ambassador: Israel is a civilized country. We recognize the orders of the court. You must promise to me that you will take only your son and will not take your property. You will not harm Andrey or his family. Some parents become violent when it comes to disputes about children. We have feedback from the FBI. They are looking for you everywhere. We cannot place you aboard a regular plane; however, we can carry you from here via a diplomatic channel. The mother-child bond is very strong. We don't want mothers to die, and you are about to do so. Israel is humanitarian country. We are returning to you your son, so that you both can live. *Shalom.*

The black limo of the Israeli Ambassador quietly parks in front of the main entrance. Nadia, who is wrapped in a yellow raincoat with large black letters that say "Secret Service," steps from the embassy. She is with a man dressed in a similar coat.

Secret Service Agent (whispering): Act cool. Don't say a word, or we are both dead.

They climb into the limo and take off. Nobody knows where Israel parks its planes. Nobody knows the time of their takeoffs or landings. It is only known that the plane left New York without incident.

Scene 2: Airplane to Israel.

The passengers inside the plane are dressed as inhabitants of Mea Sharim. They have long beards, black jackets, white stockings, and black hats with wide fields. They are sitting in their seats with books of the Torah, and all the time they are praying. Nadia puts a blanket on her head and is praying too.

She is so cold that she is shaking like a leaf. Then she suddenly feels like she is in boiling water. It becomes so hot. The sweat is running all over her body, and she becomes all wet, like a mouse in water. She tosses away the blanket and takes off her blouse.

Nadia: It's sunrise. The light is coming from everywhere. It's time to sing.

Rabbi: The lady is going insane. Cover your faces with the Torah. Pray harder. She is in the hands of the Lord now. The insane people are the People of *Hashe'm* (Hebrew for God or the One without the name). They are holy people. *Baru'ch ata' Elo hey nu.*

It feels like thousands of feathers are tickling Nadia, who begins to laugh. She is laughing very happily—like she never laughed before. Then a black cloud covers the plane. Nadia can't see the radiant light, which was so warm and kind.

Nadia: Oh, please, don't take him away from me. There is no light without my son. (*She begins to cry very bitterly.*) Phillipe! Phillipe!

She gets on her feet and begins looking for her kid all over the airplane, and she can't find him anywhere. She finds a pillow and places it in her arms like a baby. She sings lullabies and breast-feeds the pillow.

Nadia (to the praying men): Can't you be quiet? You are going to wake my baby!

She picks up a bucket with ice and begins throwing it at the passengers.

Nadia: *Ke'rach. Ke'rach* (Hebrew for ice ice).

Rabbi (raising his arms): *La Hachem* is here. *Ke'rach. Ke'rach.*

Nadia: *Achshafa't Hashma'l* (Hebrew for darkness, no electricity).

Rabbi (speaking to the pilot): Switch off all the electricity. We are in a thunderstorm. The strikes will not hit the plane when all electricity is off.

It becomes very dark. The bright lightning bolts flash in the windows and all around the plane. Suddenly, enormous hail begins pounding around all over the plane; it is falling on the seats and on the passengers. The Rabbi picks up a handful of it and places it into Nadia's hand.

Rabbi: It's diamonds.

Nadia (pouring it on the floor): I don't need diamonds. I only want my son!

The Rabbi opens the door of the plane.

Rabbi: You may go to your son now. *El Hashem* is with you. *Shalom.*

The passengers go on their knees and begin to kiss the ground. Nadia runs to a cab.

Nadia: To Jerusalem. *Be Einaim le Mishpat*, 28. As fast as you can.

Cab driver (hesitating): It's not safe to travel to Jerusalem now. There are roadside bombs, and the Arabs can stone us to death.

Nadia: Fine, then I go by foot.

Cab driver: Can you pay $100 dollars?

Nadia looks in the pockets of her coat with the letters "Secret Service." She hands him her handkerchief.

Nadia: Is that going to be enough? **Cab driver:** Yes, that's worth a fortune.

Act VI

Bethany, Jordan.

Scene 1: Outside Andrey's apartment.

The cabdriver parks next to house 28. He is pale as the snow. He opens the door of the cab, and Nadia gives him the kerchief.

Nadia: Keep the change, sir. Thank you.

She runs up the stairs and opens the door to the sitting room of the house, which she bought before going to America. She knows every stone and corner in that house, because they were all dusty and dirty and she scrubbed and scrubbed them day and night so that her husband could have the art studio.

Her library was there just as she left it. Everything was there, except for her son Phillipe.

Nadia bursts into the dining room: Andrey, his wife Eada (the Zionist beauty), and an art critic Marina are sitting at the table and drinking tea as if they are at their villa in Moscow.

Nadia: Where is my son?

Art Critic: Nadia, what a surprise! Come. Have a seat. Have some tea.

Nadia: I am asking you for the last time. Where is my son? (*She pulls a grenade from her pocket.*) I'll count to ten: one, two…

Eada rises to her feet and slides from the room like a shadow. Everybody at the table freezes and looks at the grenade in Nadia's hand. Her tiny hand holds it tightly.

Nadia: My hand will not shake. Three, four…

Eada steps back into the room. She walks in with Phillipe. She steps aside from him without saying a word. Phillipe looks exactly like in the vision, which Nadia had seen at the University. He is very quiet, and so all those who are in the room.

Nadia: Oh, my God.

She gets on her knees in front of her son and presses him to her heart. She wraps him in the Secret Service coat, picks him up in her arms, and carries him away into the streets of Jerusalem.

Phillipe: Mommy, where are we going?

Nadia: We are going to Bethany—to the monastery where we lived when I was teaching Russian there. Are you glad to see me?

Phillipe: Mommy, I thought that I would never see you again. I'm sorry that I got in a fight with that kid at our school. I'm sorry that I scratched John's truck with the knife. Can you please take me home? I'm so tired. That Halloween is so long. It's so scary. One man in a long black dress popped out across the street. He screamed, "Allah!" and then blew himself into pieces. His eyes flew across the street and fell on the ground next to me, and his blood splashed on my face. I touched his eyes, Mommy. They were not the eyes of the doll. They were human eyes, Mommy. And his blood wasn't paint. It tasted like human blood, like my blood when I cut myself.

Nadia: Honey, don't worry about John's truck. He's already forgotten about it. It's just Halloween. They just have the bigger scenery, and they stage it all to celebrate that ancient holy day. We love you, honey. We shall be back home soon. We just have to rest before the voyage. Did your daddy take you on tours and show you all the holy places and the country?

Phillipe: No. He didn't take me anywhere. I ran away from him and lived on the streets.

Nadia: Oh, my God! Where are you, God?

Phillipe and Nadia have to walk to Bethany by foot. There aren't any busses travelling at that time. Nadia wants to get a haircut for Phillipe because his hair is so long. They step into an Arabian hair salon.

Arab man: Tourists?

Nadia: Yes, we are tourists. Can you please give my son a haircut?

Arab man: Oh, yes. Sit here in that chair.

He helps Phillipe climb into the chair. Then he looks through his hair. He suddenly goes to his knees and begins to kiss the floor around the chair where Phillipe is sitting.

Arab man: Ma'am, your son's hair is all covered with lice. Your son is a Holy Child. It's not the usual lice. It's Holy Lice, which comes only to holy people. We are not allowed to touch the holy people. That's what our religion says. Therefore, I cannot touch the hair of you son, ma'am. I'm sorry, ma'am. I really am.

Phillipe: Mommy, I'll be just fine. We can get a haircut in Anchorage. (*He gracefully steps from the chair and bows to the hairstylist.*) *Saly'am.*

Phillipe and Nadia are holding hands and walking along the road from Jerusalem to Bethany. They are very happy that they have found each other again, and they talk about everything that sons and mothers talk about. The long road is running between Arabian villages. Men armed with stones and sticks are sitting on the top of the roofs on one side of the road, and United Nations soldiers in camouflage uniforms with guns are sitting on the top of the roofs on the other side.

Arab man (yelling into a megaphone): Hold your fire. It's Phillipe Habib and his mom.

Both sides are observing through the binoculars how two strange creatures are walking along the road to the monastery. The doors of the ancient monastery open for a second. Phillipe and his mom step inside. Mother Sophie seals the gates.

Palestinian: Fire.

Commander of the United Nations: Fire.

Phillipe: Mommy, where do they get so many bullets? Are they real or do they buy them from Fred Meyers? Who will be washing me if you die?

Nadia: Honey, I will never die. I always will be by your side.

Phillipe: You promise, Mommy?

Nadia: I promise, honey. I promise.

All Nadia's students, the teachers, and Mother Sophie are lined up to greet Phillipe and Nadia.

Mother Sophie: You sure grew up!

Phillipe: And so did your girls. Can we play hide and seek, like we used to do?

Mother Sophie (wiping off her tears): Yes. We are glad you came. We thought that we would never see you again.

The girls are making reverence.

The girls (in chorus in Russian): Phillipe Habib. Nadia. (*They run to Phillipe and Nadia to hug and kiss them.*) Welcome to Bethany.

Phillipe: *Saliam.*

The girls: *Saliam.*

Mother Sophie and the staff treat Phillipe and Nadia to a very nice dinner. Then they tour all over the Monastery: the chapel, which was built where Jesus resurrected Lazarus, and the headquarters of the Monastery, which was built by the last Tsar of Russia Nicholas II. The girls perform for Phillipe "Dance of the Snowflakes," by Tchaikovsky, while Mother Sophie plays the grand piano. It is really a royal reception. Phillipe smiles. It is the first smile on his exhausted and pale face, which doesn't look like the face of a child, but rather like one of a ninety-year-old man.

A very modestly dressed driver steps into the Monastery. He offers to give Phillipe a ride in a school bus over to the village of Bethany. The proposal is accepted. When they return, Phillipe is shining like the moon.

Phillipe: Mommy, it was so cool to ride in a bus. Can we do it again tomorrow?

They all go to the church, which was built across from the road. The service begins.

Phillipe: Mommy, I don't feel well. I cannot breath. Please take me outside.

Nadia picks up Phillipe and carries him into the fresh air. An Arab man with a white donkey approaches them.

Arab guide: King Abdullah sent me to escort you from the Jordanian territory. We received feedback from our informant that somebody is following you, and that somebody is very dangerous. We must leave at once.

He puts Phillipe on the donkey and begins to walk toward Jerusalem. Nadia follows them. The sun is getting very close to the field with palm trees, and the sky is turning a very deep red. They pass the last Arabian village.

Arab guide: That's as far as I can go. It's not that dark yet, and you should make it to your hotel before the night falls on the city.

Phillipe (embracing the neck of the donkey): I love you, donkey, and I want to give you a kiss. Mommy, may I kiss the donkey?

Nadia: Yes, honey.

And he does. The guide puts his right hand to his heart and bends on his knees.

Arab guide: The Great King of Jordan Abdullah appreciates the knowledge that you gave to his subjects. Your son and you will always in our prayers. *Saliam.*

The guide and the donkey disappear in the rays of the sunshine. Nadia puts Phillipe on her back, and they go back to Jerusalem. As they approach Hensemphane Garden, two men step from behind a gigantic rock. They are white men, very much American in their appearance. They are dressed in cotton shorts and short sleeve shirts of khaki color. They have photo cameras on their chests. They introduce themselves as Benjamyn and Thomas, United Nations paramedics.

Benjamyn: Ma'am, where are you going at this time of the night with a child on your back?

Nadia: We are going to Hensemphane Garden for a night. We don't have any money to pay for a hotel, and my husband will be at his office only in the morning. All offices in Alaska are closed now. We shall ask him to send us some funds and airline tickets to travel back home.

The paramedics look at Nadia as if she just fell off the moon. They look at Phillipe, who is half asleep, and then talk to each other in a whisper.

Thomas: Ma'am, we've decided to take you and your kid to the hotel contracted by the United Nations for its staff. We would like to station you in our room and give first aid to your son. He is all covered with wounds. Do you mind?

Nadia: Oh, that's so kind of you. Where are you from?

Benjamyn: From Pennsylvania.

Benjamyn takes Phillipe in his arms.

Thomas: Ma'am, can you walk or do you need me to carry you to hotel?

Nadia: What a question? Of course I can walk!

She takes a step forward and faints. It's hard to say how long she was unconscious. She comes to herself in the room in what appears to be the hotel. It is modestly furnished. There is some light coming in the windows. Two figures are standing next to the windows.

Thomas: Ma'am, we bathed your son and treated his wounds. He is sleeping now.

Nadia sees her boots, which are all covered with blood, next to her bed.

Nadia: Are these my feet?

Thomas: They're not your feet. These are your boots. We had to cut them off because your feet are swollen.

Nadia tosses away her blanket and looks at her feet. They don't look like feet at all. They are elephant feet of purple color—just a mess covered in blood.

Thomas: Ma'am, we ought to bathe your feet and apply medication. It looks like you have cellulitis.

An Arabian woman steps into the room.

Arabian woman: Ma'am, you husband is on the phone. He wants to speak to you.

She gives Nadia the receiver.

John (over the phone): Nadia, it's John. Where are you?

Nadia (looking at Benjamyn and Thomas): Where are we?

Benjamyn and Thomas: We are in Jerusalem at the hotel of the United Nations. It's morning.

Nadia: We are in Jerusalem at the hotel of the United Nations. It's morning.

John: Nadia, how did you get there?

Nadia: I don't know. I fainted, and then I woke up here. We don't have any funds, and we don't have tickets. Can you please—pretty please—get us out of here? I am about to faint again. Can you please talk to the hotel owner? Phillipe is alive. He is sleeping. (*Nadia turns to Benjamyn and Thomas.*) My husband said that he wants to speak to our son Phillipe.

Thomas picks up the phone and takes it to Phillipe.

Thomas: Hey, buddy, your daddy wants to speak to you.

Phillipe: Daddy. I love you, daddy, and I want to give you a kiss.

Thomas gives the phone to the owner of the hotel. She is crying.

Hotel owner: Yes, sir. Yes, sir. (*Then she turns to Phillipe.*) Your daddy loves you. He is going to forward the money and the airplane tickets. He will call again as soon as he makes the arrangements.

Benjamyn: Ma'am, we have to get back to our battalion. Our commander called. But we wanted to treat your feet.

Hotel owner: I can wash her feet. You have to hurry back to your battalion. It's not that close.

Thomas (to Phillipe): Bye, buddy. You take care about your mom, will you?

Phillipe (putting his arm under his cheek): My mommy is the best in the world. My daddy said that he would buy me a "Hummer" when we get home. I will send it to you for Christmas and some chocolate. Not all of it, though.

Benjamyn: Your daddy is fine. Your daddy loves you. What's his name?

Phillipe: John. His name is John.

Benjamyn (to Nadia): Ma'am, something fell off your hair.

He hands the ribbon to her. He looks as he is giving away the biggest treasure. Nadia picks up the ribbon and ties it on his sleeve.

Benjamyn (blushing): Thank you, ma'am. It's so precious.

Nadia: And so are you.

The paramedics salute and go to their jeep.

Act VII

The White House. Washington, DC.

Scene 1: The White House Presidential Office.

The honorable Senator Ted Stevens approaches the secretary of the President and requests an urgent meeting.

Secretary: The President is busy, sir.

Senator Stevens: I am busy, too. And I am not leaving until I speak to the President.

He demonstratively sits on the chair and crosses his legs. He puts his arms around his knees. He is dressed in a grey business suit with a funny tie on his neck.

Senator Stevens: What are you going to do now? Carry me from here by force? My Alaskans got trapped in Jerusalem in the middle of "antifada," and you are telling me that the President is busy. My voters called, and I am not leaving until we get them out of there.

Secretary (coming to her feet): Senator, the President will be happy to see you. You know how much he cares about Alaska and about our voters. Please.

She escorts the honorable Senator Ted Stevens into the President's office.

She seals the doors. One cannot hear their dialogue. A pale security officer steps from the office.

Security officer: Ted refused to leave the President's office until the President would carry his Alaskans from Jerusalem back to Alaska.

Secretary: But how can we do that when all the borders are sealed by the United Nations and all the airplanes are grounded?

Security officer: I don't know. Ronald said to leave them alone. They are working on the plan to rescue them. It's a kid and his mom. Her hubby is a war veteran. They say that the kid weighs only fifty pounds now, and it's a question of life or death. Right now, the President is on a direct line with the Israeli Prime Minister and his cabinet.

Secretary: Well, If It's all true, then there will be no Cabinet at all.

Security officer: Yes. It's true. The Senator has the report from the United Nations paramedics. Your hair will stand up on your head when you read it.

Secretary (with admiration): What a man! The honorable Senator Ted Stevens will stop at nothing to help his voters! I wish all our Senators were like Ted.

Mrs. Louise Johnson, the Staff Assistant from the Office of the Honorable Ted Stevens, United States Senate, steps in. She is escorted to the Presidential Office by the security officer.

Secretary: Well, what's going on?

Security officer: It's just amazing how wise are our gentlemen in Washington, DC! They are going to arrange for a Humanitarian Visa for the kid and a special rescue mission airplane with the personal pilot of United States President.

Secretary: Ronald is such a darling!

Security officer: Yes. It is very noble of him and everybody involved to put such an enormous effort into rescuing those Alaskans from the iron grip of Yasser Arafat! As the great Thomas Eliot stated: "Only those who will risk going too far can possibly find out how far one can go."

Ted Stevens and Mrs. Louise Johnson step from the President's office. Ted calls to John Koss.

Senator Stevens: John, there is good news and bad news. Which one would you like to hear? The good news is they are going to take off in a couple hours. The bad news is that they will be taking off under crossfire.

Secretary: Oh, my God, stop that plane!

Security officer: We cannot stop the airplane. The airplane always wins.

Senator Stevens: If you would excuse us, please. We have a job to do. Mrs. Johnson, follow me.

They leave. It's quiet for a moment.

Secretary: They are innocent civilian people. Can't our President stop that crossfire?

Security officer: The charging chariots don't know the ranks.

Act VIII

International Christian Embassy. Jerusalem, Israel.

"But if some of the branches were broken off, and you, being a wild olive were grafted in among them and became partaker with them of the rich root of the olive tree, do not be arrogant toward the branches; but if you are arrogant, remember that it is not you who supports the root, but the root supports you" (Romans 11:17,18).

Scene 1: International Christian Embassy.

The International Christian Embassy is used as a catalyst in the reconciliation between Christians, Hebrew people, and Arab people. The Christian Embassy Network covers the spiritual, political, philosophical, and economical needs of the modern inhabitants of the region. The Embassy is located in Jerusalem, and all staff work on a volunteer basis.

Nadia worked for four years for the International Christian Embassy as an interpreter. She also carried a lot of medical and food supplies, which were distributed equally among the Hebrew and Arab families. She was always carrying Phillipe in her arms everywhere she went, and jointly they were giving love and support to a lot of desperate people, who gave Phillipe the nickname "Phillipe Habib." The three-year-old blonde was fluent in English, Hebrew, and Arabic and actively participated in humanitarian projects.

Phillipe and Nadia go to the Embassy to say goodbye to their friend, Mr. Jan Willem van der Hoeven, the chief speaker of the Embassy. The usually white building is covered with black paint, like the rest of Jerusalem. It is very depressing to be among that blackness. Even twenty years later, the aftershock of that psychological horror endures. Unlike other establishments, which are all closed, the Embassy is open. The secretary in her white blouse is sitting as usual at her desk covered by newsletters, prayers, and brochures. She is just pale, more than usual. They never need an appointment. As the personal interpreter of the chief speaker, Nadia has the privilege to step into his office any time.

Jan is dressed in white shirt and black slacks. He is wearing a tie, as he always does. It's as if nothing has changed, as if they always were here. Jan embraces Phillipe and Nadia like his own family, and they first pray, like they always do.

Jan: We thought that we never would see you again.

Nadia: It's all in the hands of our Lord. *Commen't elle vous?*

Jan (smiling): *Tout va bien, Mon Generale.*

He always calls Nadia Mon Generale, *as part of his respect and appreciation for her work for the embassy.*

Jan: I hope that Phillipe enjoyed the bus tour over Bethany, which King Abdullah gave to him. He stated that Phillipe Habib was *tres noble aux respectoma.'*

Phillipe: *Merci. Je woudre le voir les penteurs. Excuse moi. He gracefully steps from the room.*

Jan: *Vous ette fatigue, mais sharmante.* I really think that you and Phillipe should not travel across the Atlantic now. It's such long and dangerous flight. You are both too young to die.

Nadia: "Even the hair will not fall off your head, if you believe in me," said Our Lord Jesus.

Jan: I called to Yasser Arafat and asked him to hold the fire when your plane takes off…

Nadia: What did he say?

Jan: He made a pathetic speech on behalf of the hardship of Palestinian children…hard conditions at their schools and lack of the teachers and school supplies…and he said that he liked the TPR (Total Physical Respond) method, which you introduced to the boys and schools. He said that you look like the sister of his wife Gale'ana. You are not her sister, are you?

Nadia: The weather is nice today, isn't it?

Jan: *Vie, c'est sa, Mon Generale.*

Nadia: Are they going to hold the fire?

Jan: He said that he would give me an answer pretty soon.

A Molotov cocktail flies through the window into the office. It sets fire to the curtains at the window. The secretary runs in with the phone in her hands.

Secretary: It's Yasser Arafat. He asks if you have received his answer.

Jan (trying to stop the spreading fire with his jacket): Is there anything else he asks?

The secretary bites her lower lips. She is hesitant to speak further.

Jan: Well, what else did he ask?

Secretary: He asked, "Where was Your Lord when my men blew up the church in Bethany?"

Jan: When did they do it?

Secretary: About ten minutes ago. A priest and two nuns were killed. Some of the girls were wounded. King Abdullah drove them in his bus to his palace for their safety.

Another Molotov cocktail falls into the hall.

Jan: It's getting hot in here. It looks we are going to have a major offensive from Monsieur Arafat.

Nadia picks the phone from the secretary.

Nadia: Meseur Arafat? *Bon nair. She dials the number.*

Nadia: *Arie, Tychva medaberet* (Hebrew for Hope is speaking). Cover me. *Shalom.*

Jan: Whom did you just call, *Mon Generale*?

Nadia: I called our bodyguard.

Jan: A bodyguard! Who is your bodyguard?

Nadia: Ariel Sharon.

The Israeli artillery launches massive rockets that shower on the headquarters of Arafat for the next two hours. French journalists ask, "What is the cause for such an intense attack? The chief speaker of the International Christian Embassy mysteriously says, "Shershe' La Famme (French for 'Look for the woman')."

Men of the famous Goani Brigade of the Israel Defense Force receive a Bible, a rifle, and an arm badge on completion of their assignment.

"And so, the yearning song with which these will long"" Shall far outpass the power of human telling;

For none can guess its grace, till he becomes the place Wherein the Holy Spirit makes His dwelling.

Act IX

Knesset. Jerusalem, Israel.

Scene 1

Knesset, the office of the Prime Minister of Israel.Modestly furnished, the office is radiant with dignity. Portraits of Hertzel and Bengurion are placed next to the portrait of Menachem Begin. The photograph of the Israeli Prime Minister Golde Meir stands on the writing desk. There are three telephones of different colors: one for the White House, one for the minister of defense, and one for the wife of the Premiere. He is sitting at the desk and reading The Jerusalem Post. Nobody can see his face. Ariel Sharon quietly opens the door. He carries a tray with tea, lime drops, and honey. He solemnly places the tray in front of the Prime Minister. The Premier continues to read the newspaper and stirs the tea with a tiny silver spoon.

Arie: I wanted to ask your permission to drive to the American Embassy. I would like to request from their designated official the code for the anti- missile defense. I would like our Air Force to take off and cover the American civilian airplane, which has been dispatched to Tel Aviv under personal orders of Ronald Reagan.

The Premier: Arie, I hope you know what you are doing. The boy is not Jewish.

Arie jumps to the table like the lion. He pulls off the tablecloth. The tea and the lime drops spill on the Persian carpet. He smacks his fist on the table, and it cracks.

Arie: The boy is an Israeli citizen. And if we can carry from that hell at least one Israeli child, then I will fight for it till my final breath.

A Molotov cocktail flies through the window into the office; it sets fire to the curtains at the window. The Premier continues to read the newspaper.

The Premier: Pardon me for saying this, sir, but I think that you are over the hill in love with the boy's mother.

Arie: Guard, carry to safety the Prime Minister now. Evacuate all children into the dungeons. Put your best suits on and dispatch the Prime Minister's limo to that boy, Phillipe Reznitsky, and his mom.

Arie straightens his uniform and solemnly places his right hand on his heart.

Arie: Israel, as a country, doesn't know any other Caesar except for the President of the United States. Arie Sharon doesn't know any other woman in his life, except of his wife. You must be of very high opinion of me to think I can have compassion for a non-Jewish woman. *Hus vai haleala vae shalom.* What about permission to drive to the American Embassy?

The Premier: The permission is granted, and so is my signature to appoint you our next prime minister. Sorry if I hurt your feelings, Arie. There are rumors that you carry her photograph in the pocket of your uniform. You should surrender it to me now. *S'est tune scandal.*

Arie rips off his pocket and puts the female's picture into the palm of the Prime Minister. He covers his face with his headgear and runs from the office to his jeep. The Premier opens his palm and looks at the photograph, which turns out to be the photo of Golde Meir.

Prime Minister: I'll be damned.

The guards whisk him to the shelter via the kitchen.

Arie jumps into his jeep and tells the driver to take him to the American Embassy. It's under fire from Molotov cocktails. He is trying to find the office of the designated official, who is in the possession of the access code for the anti-missile defense. As they find the office, they see a young man sitting at the table with his head on the desk.

Arie: This is not a time to have a nap.

The man does not respond. Arie comes to him and taps him on the shoulder. There is no response. Arie turns his head and sees that the man is dead. He looks almost like a child—probably on his first assignment after graduation.

The Embassy secretary steps in. She is in a white blouse, covered by glass and blood. She is emotionally shaken, but firm. She is holding in her hands a shredding machine.

Arie: Is there anybody else at the Embassy who is knowledgeable about the anti-missile code?

Embassy secretary: He was the only one. If you would excuse me, please, I have to shred the confidential documents.

She steps from the office.

Arie (turning to his driver): Take all the wives and the sons of the American diplomats and put them aboard that plane. Take all their daughters, dress them as the Palestinians, and hide them in the dungeons of the old city.

The American counselor runs to Ariel Sharon.

American (outraged): You have no legal right to take my wife and son and put them aboard that plane!

Arie: I am the minister here, and I make the rules!

Embassy secretary (stepping between the American and Arie): One little boy asks if he can take his Teddy Bear with him?

The counselor looks at Arie. Arie looks at the counselor.

Arie and the American counselor (together): Yes.

Act X

International Airport
of Ben Gurion. Tel-Aviv, Israel.

Scene 1: Arabean Hotel, Jerusalem

Phillipe is sitting on an antique bench in a tiny garden. The table next to him has a plate with grapes. Phillipe is eating the grapes and watching the Arabian dancers, who perform in front of him an exquisite, ancient dance. A man dressed as a servant in ancient Egypt is waving a feather fan in the air around Phillipe. The Israeli police cover the entire roof of the police station and are watching the scene through binoculars.

Police officer 1: What are they doing?

Police officer 2: The kid is eating grapes, and the women are dancing. His dad is a friend of the President: *Amerykai.* Ariel Sharon called and ordered us to keep them safe. He said that, if even one hair falls from the head of Phillipe Habib, we are all going to be dead.

Benjamyn and Thomas, who are dressed in camouflage uniforms, step into the garden. They pick up Phillipe and toss him into the air. Phillipe claps his hands. A smile appears on his pale face: He is very glad to see his friends.

Benjamyn comes to Nadia and bends his head.

Benjamym: Ma'am, would you like to dance?

Thomas imitates Benjamin and invites Phillipe. They are all dancing. It is romantic. The petals of the flowers are flying into the garden. They cover them like the snow.

Police officer 1: What are they doing?

Police officer 2: They are dancing.

Police officer 1: In the middle of "Antifada"? Americans! Only they can do it! And how we are supposed to protect them from the snipers? Or Molotov cocktails—when they dance?

The black limo of the Israeli Prime Minister parks next to the hotel. Israeli security steps from the limo: They are wearing elegant black suits and white gloves. Thomas steps from the garden and walks toward the limo. He is carrying Phillipe in his arms. Benjamyn walks to the limo with Nadia next to him. Israeli security opens the doors of the limo. They place Phillipe and Nadia inside. Then they buckle them and sit next to them. Thomas bends to the window.

Thomas: Bye, Phill! Are you going to write me to Pennsylvania?

Phillipe: Yes.

Benjamyn (bending to the window): Nadia, may I write to you in Alaska?

Nadia: Yes.

Security seals the windows. The limo takes off. The hotel staff and the dancers go on their knees and begin to pray.

Scene 2: Hensemphane Garden.

The artist Andrey Resnitsky, dressed in a white shirt, is standing on the leather and painting "The Last Supper." The priest and the nuns are holding the brushes. The artist Dina storms inside.

Dina: Andrey, they are taking off. They are taking off under crossfire!

Andrey tears off his shirt into pieces.

Andrey: *Eled Shely, Phillipe!*

Tears are running along his face. He picks up dust and puts it on his head.

Andrey: Oh, my God, what have I done?

The priest and the nuns go on their knees and begin to pray.

Scene 3: Airport.

The limo arrives to the airport. Security escorts Phillipe and Nadia to the airplane. They step on the stairs.

Security guard: If they shoot you down, we don't know anything about it.

Nadia is holding in her arms her son. She has, with her, her biggest treasure—her child.

Nadia: We are really tired; we ought to have some rest. Thank you for your hospitality. *Shalom.*

The plane stands solemnly for a moment. Then it begins to drive along the runway and suddenly takes off into the air. It flies higher and higher into the sky. And soon it looks like a bird.

Palestinian Commander: Fire!

United Nations Commander: Fire!

Phillipe: Mommy, look! What nice firecrackers!

The Palestinians simultaneously begin their attack on the Israeli settlements, Haifa and Tel-Aviv, from the air. There are more rockets and bombs than the trees on the ground. It looks like an ocean of fire. It looks like hell on Earth. Rockets are flying all around the plane, and they can be seen through the window. They look like tiny red lines—something that you put between missing words in a sentence.

Dark clouds cover the plane. Phillipe is sleeping on the chest of his mom.

He is warm and comfortable. He sees his friend Frank. They splash in the pond, and Frank's grandma is chasing them with a slipper.

Act XI

Elmendorf Air Force Base. Alaska.

Scene 1: Air Force base.

The plane lands without the incident. Paramedics and fire trucks look like toys under the snow. Crying family members are running toward the children and women stepping from the plane. Not far from the building is standing a man in a camouflage raincoat. It is John.

John: Yes, Margaret. The plane is here. She will be in class with the students tonight. I assume she had a great vacation and plenty of rest. Yes, you will make it through the semester. I don't know how they look, but I will. Yes, I will call you when we arrive home.

Miss Mary, the teacher of Phillipe at his elementary school, steps into the class.

Scene 2: Classroom.

Miss Mary: Children, Phillipe is back home. We should write greeting cards for him and make a tape with our wishes for him. He is coming to class tomorrow.

The children jump on their feet and begin to embrace each other.

Children (chanting in chorus): Phillipe! Phillipe! Phillipe!

Scene 3: Federal Aviation.

Mrs. Charlene Derry, the Director of the Department of Liaison (Intern. Negotiations), runs into the conference room of Federal Aviation and informs the Russian Delegation.

Charlene: Our interpreter and her son Phillipe are back home. We shall resume our negotiations as scheduled. The flying routes between Alaska and Anadyr will be opened as scheduled. (*She smiles to the Head of the Russian Delegation.*) Under your wise supervision, of course. *Spa Seabo* (Russian for thank you). How is my Russian?

The pilot, Phillipe, and Nadia get off the plane. They slowly begin to walk towards the man in the raincoat.

Pilot: Here is your boy, sir.

John (handing Nadia her file): Here is your schedule, honey.

Nadia: Gosh, John. It's about twenty-five tons! You have no heart, John!

John (saluting to Phillipe): How are you, sir? Welcome home.

Phillipe (saluting back to him): I'm fine, Sir.

John turns to the pilot. His gray eyes are smiling, and his face—the face of the soldier with the scars from the battles—is shining like the moon.

John: What's your name, son?

The pilot is very shy. He takes off his headgear and squashes it in his hands.

Pilot: Federico Garcia Lorca.

John: I'll be damned!

Documentary

Drawings, Photography, Letters, and Newspaper Articles

March 26, 1990

Honorable
Ted Stevens

United States
Senate
Washington,
DC 20510

Dear Senator Stevens,

I want to express my gratitude to you and your staff for the efforts and assistance provided on behalf of my son, Phillipe, to allow him to return back home to Alaska.

Phillipe was born in Moscow, USSR, under a hunger strike during our struggle for exit visas. This case was presented in the world press (1979– 1980) as "The Soviet Catch 22." It was my son's first battle for the ideals of freedom and democracy, the ideals that America has stood for since the first days of its existence. During the years of immigration, the life of this child was not a bed of roses, but he did not complain; he believed in God and America.

I am grateful that you did not let him down, and that people representing the State of Alaska expressed concern for an Alaskan family and its needs. I believe that Phillipe will be a good citizen and will stand up for this state, like you and your people stood up for him, and like you stand up for all Alaskans who have entrusted you to represent this beautiful state.

As a mother, and as an Alaskan resident, I thank you, Senator, and your office staff for the humanitarian concern and a job excellently done.

Thank you for your help.

With much respect,

Nadejda M. Phillips

March 26, 1990

Louise Johnson Staff Assistant Office of the Honorable Ted Stevens United States Senate Washington, DC 20510

Dear Ms. Johnson,

I would like to personally thank you for the assistance you have provided on behalf of my son, Phillipe Reznitsky, to obtain parole authorization to return to the State of Alaska, which has been his home for the past four years.

Phillipe loves Alaska, his American father, his friends, and his toys. It was crucial for this child's world to be back in normal, humane conditions and for him to return home. I am grateful that you did not treat this case formally and that you put so much time and enormous effort to make this child happy.

There are many different ways to express gratitude and to write letters of gratification. I don't want to write you a standard letter because I am sure you receive hundreds of them from the many people in need of help who apply to your office for help, but few write to express their actual feelings.

I am so grateful that I feel like crying, and I am. These are happy tears that are running along my face and out of my heart. They are my first happy tears in America, and I am not ashamed.

They claim in the history books that America has been discovered. It is not true because I discover this beautiful land every day, with every person I meet. I never thought in Jerusalem, during the dark days of antifada, far away from Washington DC, that I would meet and be as kindly assisted by a person like you. I am grateful to my Lord and this United States Government that I was granted such a privilege.

God bless you and God bless America.

Thank you for your humanitarian concern and your help.

With much respect,

Nadejda M. Phillips

March 26, 1990

Honorable Ted Stevens US Senator for Alaska United States Senate Washington, DC 20510-6025

Dear Senator Stevens,

I want to personally thank you and your staff member Louise Johnson for the concern you showed and the help your office gave in working with the immigration people in Washington so that my paperwork was completed to allow me to return back home here to Alaska. I love Alaska and you and the people in Alaska. Thank you again very much.

Sincerely,
Phillipe Reznitsky
8301 Range
View Ave.
Anchorage,
AK 99504

About the Artist

The displayed landscapes "Village Arabe" have been created under the wise supervision of the Prime Minister Menachem Begin. They have been successfully presented in *Israel* and *France*. The landscapes were made in a very complex technique: pastel.

The portrait "Repose" by Mr. Reznitsky won first prize in a worldwide contest made by the Royal Academy of Portraits in London, England.

The artist was commissioned to paint the only oil portrait of the Prime Minister of Israel, which remains the National Treasure of Israel.

STD.DD ISBN #0-8059-6593-9
Order your book via:
Nadia Herndon PO Box 203343
Anchorage AK 99520-334343

Family History

Family Tree

The blood that courses through my veins is of British and Russian origin, though it can be traced to Viking, Slav, Mongolian, and perhaps Persian roots. I am attempting to trace all my roots as far as possible and produce a reference work for generations to follow. Any input available from visitors to this page will be welcome. My family on both the maternal and paternal sides can be traced back well over 600 years. Many ancestors on the paternal side have been integral to the history and development of Russia, particularly the Ukraine, and are remembered to this day. On the paternal side, the significant names that make up my heritage are as follows (dates indicated are documented traces researched so far):

Apostol 1630–
Khlopov 1795–
Korobyine 1377–

Mouravieff (or Muraviev) 1488–
Mouravieff-Apostol (or Muraviev-Apostol) 1800–
Tereschenko 1795–

The maternal side finds its roots in Norse origins with the first invasion of the British Isles by the Vikings and their settlements in the Isle of Man. The names associated with this lineage include the following:

Hall 1803–
Caine 1730–
Hall Caine 1853–

The Russian Side

My Russian heritage can perhaps be traced back in several directions to *Rurik* in the north, *Genghis Khan* and the Golden Horde in the east, and *Sekivan Kotchu-Bey* in the south. Thus, my family tree most probably has roots incorporating the three primary influences on *Russia*: the Vikings, the Mongols, and the Ottomans.

The Mouravieff Descendancy

Rurik, regarded as the first of the *Rus* and the origin of the name given to *Russia*, was born about 810 and died about 879. His origin is thought to be Scandinavian or possibly Jutland (present-day Denmark) from a Viking clan, an offshoot of the Varangians. There are differing theories as to whether he and his clan invaded the area of *Kiev*, or whether he was invited in to provide security as a mercenary force against invaders attempting to disrupt the lucrative trading activities centered in Novgorod on the Volkhov River. In any case, his kinsman Oleg founded the grand principality of Kiev and was succeeded by Prince Rurik's son *Igor* (912–945), who is considered to be the real founder of the Russian princely house. The descendants of *Igor* established, among other princely houses, those of Moscow and Tver. The *Mouravieffs* are allegedly descendants of *Yaroslav* (Grand Prince of *Vladimir* 1264–1271), and actual records of them have been documented as early as 1488. The *Mouravieff* name is often associated with high-ranking military and diplomatic posts. A *Mouravieff*led Russian conquests include Poland under Catherine the Great, the establishment of the Amur and Ussuri Rivers as the boundary with China in 1858, and the founding of Vladivostok in 1860. The Amursky Peninsula, a large peninsula in Siberia where Vladivostok is situated, is named to this day after Nicolai Muraviev, who was given the title of Count Amursky. The Mouravieff name is also closely associated with the Decembrist uprising in 1825 against Tsar Nicholas I. In 1761, Ivan Mouravieff married the only daughter of Peter Apostol, the son of Hetman Daniel Apostol. In 1800, at the request of Peter, Ivan's son Matvei agreed to attach the Apostol name to his own to prevent the Apostol family name from dying out. Thus was born the name Mouravieff-Apostol.

The Apostol Descendancy

In 1238, a *Mongol* army under Batu, grandson of *Genghis Khan*, invaded Rus and in 1240 captured *Kiev*. It was ransacked many times over the ensuing 100 years by the Tatars based in the Crimea. It is most probable that the *Apostol* family has its roots in the Crimea and served as the Khan's representative ruling over regions to the south and east of Kiev. Indeed, the word "Apostol" in Russian means "designated Chief of the conquered nation." These feudal states were headed by a Hetman who was elected by the various tribal chiefs. The first documented *Apostol* is *Paul*, who was born about 1630. His son, the Hetman Daniel, was born in 1654 and died in 1737. This was the Hetman Period in Ukraine's history. His father or grandfather probably helped the Cossacks capture *Kiev* in 1648 and then, under increasing military pressure from the Polish, offered their allegiance to Moscow under Tsar Peter the Great. The Treaty of Andrusovo in 1667 concluded the absorption of the Ukraine west of the Dnieper into the Russian Empire as an autonomous Cossack state under the protection of Moscow. By 1686, Kiev became part of Russia, and under Catherine the Great in 1793, the Ukraine east of the Dnieper River had also joined the Russian Empire. Daniel Apostol was the last of the Hetman (Ataman) warlords and was elected from the city of Glouchov, though his residence was in Homoutetz near Mirgorod and the village of Poltava. He built his church at Velikii-Sorochintzi, made famous by the 19th century poet Gogol. His rule ended in 1725. Little is known of his son Peter except that Peter's daughter Elena, the last surviving *Apostol*, married Ivan Mouravieff in 1761, and Peter later requested their son *Ivan* to add the name *Apostol*, so that the *Apostol* family name would live on.

The Hlopov Descendancy

Nothing is known of this family prior to *Nadjde* (affectionately known as Baboushka) marrying Theodore *Tereschenko* in 1883. Their daughter would then marry Vladimir *Mouravieff-ApostolKorobyine*, my grandfather. Family tradition passed down, however, suggests that this wealthy family in *Kiev* could trace its lineage back to King Pepin III the Short of France, father of Charlemagne (721 AD). Since Pepin III expanded his empire considerably and exchanged ambassadors with the Byzantine Emperor and the Caliphate of Baghdad, it is reasonable that some of his descendants could have settled in the easternmost parts of his empire.

The Tereschenko descendancy

This family first appears in *Kiev* during the 18th century, and the first recorded ancestor is Artemyi *Tereschenko*, father of Theodore *Tereschenko*. *Theodore* and his brother, *Nikola*, contributed huge sums of money to the development of *Kiev* and many of its institutions. Nikola's daughter Barbara married Bogdan *Hanenko*, and together they established a collection of art in the Hanenko Museum of Kiev, financed in large part by the couple's father and uncle. The collection is now housed in two parts in the restored mansions of *Nikola* and *Theodore Tereschenko* located in *Kiev* on Boulevard Tereschenko.

The Mouravieff-Apostol Descendancy

The first *Mouravieff-Apostol* was *Matvei*, son of *Ivan Mouravieff*, who at the request of *Peter Apostol* added the name *Apostol* to that of *Mouravieff*. His marriage to Anna Tchernoevitch resulted in a daughter, *Katerina*, and three sons, *Matvei*, *Sergei*, and *Hipolyte*. The sons became leaders in the Decembrist movement of 1825, which was crushed by Tsar Nicholas I, resulting in Matvei being banished to Siberia, Sergei being hanged, and Hipolyte losing his life to a gunshot wound that some say was self-inflicted. Matvei was eventually allowed to return to his homeland and had his honor reinstated by Tsar Alexander II in 1885. During his last years, he befriended Vladimir *Korobyine*, his sister *Katerina's* grandson. Katerina married a Bibikof, and their daughter married Vladimir's father. Having no children to carry on the name of *Mouravieff-Apostol*, Matvei requested Vladimir *Korobyine* add the name to his. In 1886, by decree of the Tsar, *Vladimir Korobyine* became *Vladimir Mouravieff-Apostol-Korobyine*. He married Nadya Tereschenkov and had three sons, Vadim, Andrew (my father), and Alexis. Vadim died in 1999, and Alexis died in 2000. Andrew had three sons, Michael, Christopher, and me. Andrew died in 2002.

The Korobyine Descendancy

The *Korobyine* family name has been traced back to *Selivan Kotchu-Bey* in Constantinople, who lived from about 1377 to 1463. The *Bey* was a title of authority given to rulers of different tribes roaming the Anatolian steppes and other parts of the Ottoman Empire. Apparently, the *Kotchu-Bey* name became corrupted or changed such that his son became known as *Ivan Selivanovitch Korobia*. By about 1482 with the birth of his son, *Ivan Ivanovitch*, the name *Korobia* had become *Korobyine*. Little is known of the family's exploits, though the lineage is well documented. *Vladimir Korobyine* (1826– 1895) married *Katerina Bibikov*. It was their son, *Vladimir* (my grandfather), at the request of the famed Decembrist, *Matvei Mouravieff-Apostol*, who added the name *Mouravieff-Apostol* by decree of Tsar Alexander II to his own to create the current family name of *Mouravieff-Apostol-Korobyine*.

The Manx side

Of Celt or probably Viking ancestry, this is the maternal side of my heritage.

The Hall Caine Descendancy

The Caines of the Isle of Man can be traced back for many generations. My ancestors for whom we have direct records start with William Caine, who was born around 1730. He had several children, including a namesake son William. He in turn reared a large family, with one son being named John. Due to the poor economic conditions in the Isle of Man in these times and the fact that the family had lost all their property, which they had used for farming, John went to Liverpool, England to earn a living. It was there where Thomas, the most famous of the Caines, was born.

Sir Hall Caine, born Thomas Henry Hall Caine, was a colorful personage famed for his many novels about the Isle of Man. His books, published between 1877 and 1931, were translated into dozens of languages and often reached more than twenty re-printings. For his work during the First World War, he was knighted Sir Hall Caine. This was unusual since most such titles include only the first name. Apparently,

Sir Hall Caine disliked his given name of Thomas and convinced the King to bestow his title using only his last names.

He had two sons, Gordon Ralph and Derwent, who served in Parliament with distinction, and Derwent was also knighted and received a baronet. Derwent had at least three children out of wedlock, one of whom (Eline) was subsequently adopted by the elder Sir Hall Caine as his own daughter. Gordon Ralph had a son Derek and a daughter Mary, my mother. Eline married Charles Gill and had a daughter Gloria, who married a well- known American television financial analyst, Luis Ruckheyser.

They had three daughters and lived in the United States. Eline died in 1999. Derek, who died in 2004, had a daughter Melissa, who now lives in New York. Mary had two sons, Michael and Nicholas, who live in New York and Florida. Mary died in December of 2003 in Florida. More information on this illustrious family can be found at the Hall Caine website.

Miss Nadia Herndon.
The author of "Antifada". Chena Hot Springs. Alaska

Mr. John Koss & Miss Nadia Phillip.
The parents of Sir Phillipe Reznitsky

"Sir Phillipe A. Reznitsky (Né Muraviev-Apostol)
Anchorage, Alaska. The legal owner of the largest, nuclear shipyard in the
world "Sórmovo-Krásnoe", Russia.

Pepsi's Little people I.D. card with the photo
of Sir Phillipe Reznitsky at the time of his voyage to Jerusalem

MENACHEM BEGIN, PRIME MINISTER OF ISRAEL   מנחם בגין ראש ממשלת ישראל

Colored photo of the portrait of the Prime Minister of Israel
by Sir. Andrey Reznitsky. Circa 1982. Oil on canvas.

The colored photo of the location, where Miss Nadia Phillips had the vision of her son being in critical conditions in Jerusalem

The colored photo of the house of the family, from where
Miss Nadia's pilgrimage to Jerusalem to resque her son: Began

PHILLIPE-HABIB   BY NadiaHerNd.

Gethsemane Garden: Benjamine & Thomas

In The Face of Jinn
May Book Club Selection

American sisters Christine and Elizabeth Shepherd are on a buying trip in India for their California import business when Elizabeth suddenly disappears. Christine challenges the ineffectual U.S. and Indian bureaucracies and ventures alone into Afghanistan and Pakistan where foreigners are prohibited and women are sequestered.

In search of her sister, and disguised in the traditional female garb of Islam, Christine finds herself caught in a web of terrorism as she navigates the mysterious tribes of the Pashtuns, has a dangerous encounter with the Taliban, falls into a forbidden love, and learns to fear the "Jinn," the devils that dominate the superstitions of the people she must understand in order to survive.

Author Cheryl Howard Crew's rich detail and keen observation lend an authenticity to her fiction that vividly brings to life a region many Americans know little about." -- Orlando Sentinel

"A thrill ride of twists, turns, and sudden fear that doesn't let go until the last page." – Jean M. Auel

"Impressive...Winning and intensely moving." – Kirkus Reviews

Everyone is invited to attend a discussion of In The Face of Jinn. For more information, contact Charlotte Pendleton at 343-2996 or pendletoncl@muni.org.
Saturday, May 20, 3pm
Loussac, Ann Stevens Room, Level 3

End of long lines at Loussac?

State-of-the-art self-check machines are being installed at Loussac and the five branch libraries of Anchorage Municipal Libraries in May. Besides being located near the circulation desks of the libraries, one machine will be placed in the media section at Loussac to facilitate quick checkout for our patrons.

Regular Features @ Loussac

Friends of the Library Board Meeting
Monthly meeting. Alden Todd Board Room, Loussac, Level 4.
Wednesday, May 10, 5:30pm.

Library Advisory Board Meeting
Monthly meeting. Samson-Dimond Branch Library, Dimond Mall, **Wednesday, May 17, 5:30pm.**

Genealogy Assistance
Anchorage Genealogical Society volunteers assist people researching their family heritage. Loussac, Level 3, Wednesdays, 1-2pm. In summer, check with reference librarians to find out when volunteers are available.

Friends of the Library Gift Shop @ Loussac

FIND THE PERFECT GIFT FOR MOTHER'S DAY!!

Purchases support Anchorage Municipal Libraries.

AURORA Coffee Co.
Your Cafe @ Loussac

Summer Daze
16oz Mocha Glacier
Only $3
Save 75 cents

Hours: Mon-Thu 9am-9pm/ Fri & Sat 9am-6pm/Sun 12-5pm

Original invitation for the reception at "Captain Cook Hotel", where the first part of the book begins. There is a great photo of Phillipe there at the time of his dialogue with the "White House" on behalf of the reception at the "Captain Cook Hotel"

"Four Exhibits grace Loussac during May". It was visited by 5,000 people. It was at Ann Stevens Room at Loussac Library as the enormous effort of Sir Phillipe A. Reznitsky to give the better Education to the people, to support the memory of Mrs. Ann Stevens, the wife of the Honorable Senator Ted Stevens.